Old Crail
Eric Eunson

Junior members of the Crail Operatic Society photographed in Marketgate opposite the Diamond Jubilee Fountain in 1911.

© Eric Eunson, 2007
First published in the United Kingdom, 2007,
by Stenlake Publishing Ltd.
www.stenlake.co.uk
ISBN 9781840334081

The publishers regret that they cannot supply
copies of any pictures featured in this book.

Rose Wynd in 1910.

Eric Eunson would like to express grateful thanks to Crail Preservation Society for their help with reseach.

INTRODUCTION

In 1997 Mesolithic waste pits were excavated at Fife Ness, and these were found by experts to date back some 9,500 years, just after the end of the last ice age. They were the earliest evidence so far recorded of human habitation on mainland Scotland, and antedating the already impressive historic pedigree of the area around Crail. An abundance of finds at Crail and elsewhere in the East Neuk show the area was the scene of extensive Bronze Age activity.

It stretches the imagination not at all to suggest the Crail district would have been well known to St. Cainneach, a 6th century Irish missionary monk. He was St. Columba's interpreter among the Picts and the traditional founder of the church at Kilrymont, which became St. Andrews Cathedral. The 8th century Sauchope Stone affirms the Christianity of the area by that date. Fife Ness is traditionally regarded as the place where Constantine, the great Christian ruler of Pictish Fife and Tayside, was brutally murdered in a cave by Viking marauders, an event said to have taken place in 874.

The name Crail is thought to derive from *caer* - a fort, and *ela* - a corner, and appears in many forms in old records including Karaill and Karal. Crail does not feature on a map of the 10th century, but does on one from the 12th, by which time it was a place of some importance. Tradition maintains that Crail was created a royal burgh by David I (1123-54) and while the original charter has long since perished, there is no reason to dispute the verity of this statement. David I certainly had a favoured residence in the town, the site of which is commemorated by the Castle Walk. Scottish physician and antiquary Sir Robert Sibbald describes the ruins of the castle as still being visible in 1710. The earliest burgh charter dates from 1310 in the reign of Robert the Bruce, but is probably just a confirmation of the original.

During David's reign Crail became a constabulary, and obtained the right to customs dues extending from the middle of the River Leven to Putikin (Pitmilly). The important royal connection with the area is commemorated in the names of Kingsmuir, Kingsbarns, and the King's Mills which once stood near the east end of the Castle Walk. It is also noted there was a keeper of the King's rabbit warren, who had an annual salary of 16s 8d in 1264.

It is probable the feudal overlords of Crail were Anglo-Normans settled here in the time of David l, the first of whom named is Adam de Cairyll noted in 1227. The barony of Crail was granted to Richard de Belo Monte in the reign of Alexander III (1249-86). In 1294 his successor Isabella de Bello Monte was granted permission by the occupying King Edward l to hold a market in the burgh.

The Church of Crail was gifted to the Culdees in the 11th century and when this order of the old Celtic church was displaced in the 12th century, its revenues passed to the Cistercian Convent of Haddington. In 1177 it commanded a stipend of 80 merks, equal second on the list of churches extant in east Fife at that time. In 1515 there were five chaplainries located in the church, that is altars each with their own salaried chaplain. These were swept away by Knox's reformers in 1559, along with the destruction of many precious holy objects and books, of which only a list survives today. In 1587 the revenues of the parish Church were transferred to the administration of the burgh.

In the tax roll of the Convention of Royal Burghs in 1575 Crail rates 5th of the 12 comparable burghs in Fife. This is more impressive than it appears, for Crail is being compared here with other places with extensive coal and salt industries. At this convention Crail affirmed its rights and privileges from Leven to Pitmilly, which were much resented in the other towns and villages (Crail had attempted to deny Pittenweem the right to hold markets or levy its own customs). In 1587 Thomas Dishington of Elie obtained the erection of Elie into a free port, on the conditions that cargoes from Elie and Crail would be mutually exempt from duty and Crail would receive an annual payment from Elie. A similar solution was applied between Crail and Pittenweem, although these annual duties were still payable to Crail until the 19th century.

From the 12th century onwards Crail developed as a mercantile burgh, trading most notably with the Flemish and Dutch, The church bell of 1614 was cast in Holland and bears a Dutch inscription, while the local pantiles are of a form copied from cargoes of similar tiles which arrived as ballast on Dutch trading vessels.

Fishing beyond immediate domestic supply was not carried out on the Forth to any great extent before the 17th century, so mention of herring being carried from Crail to Clackmannan in 1343 is a significant early record of commercial fishing. By the early 18th century fishing was the main industry of Crail, when local boats were joined by 100s hundreds from Angus, the Mearns and Aberdeen. These were supplied with nets by the local inhabitants, for which they were paid with a percentage of the catch. Almost the whole economy was based on fishing or ancillary trades, but by 1790 the industry had endured 50 years of decline, and it was remarked "The whole town bears evident marks of having seen better days." The burgh at that time still boasted six sloops of 20-25 tons and a 150 ton brig engaged in commercial transport.

Agriculture in the parish was also backward at this time, with little land enclosure or artificial drainage in place, and in 1790 the Revd. Bell was moved to describe the farm houses in the parish as "hovels". However, by 1845 things were much improved and it was reported that few householders did not keep a pig for domestic use and that "in few places are the farm steadings so good and the accommodation for man and beast so ample."

Crail had a population of 1,652 in 1801 and this rose to 1,931 by the census of 1861, but declined to 1,704 by 1891. The harbour was too small to accommodate the larger vessels necessary for the offshore herring fishing after the middle of the 19th century, although there were pipe dreams that Roome Bay might be made into a large harbour. The absence of a rail link until 1883 also proved an impediment to Crail's economy.

The arrival of the railway set in motion the rebirth of Crail as a summer resort. In 1889 there were still many pockets of decay and derelict buildings in the main streets of the burgh, but within a decade all had been improved or swept away, as villas, hotels and boarding houses were erected for wealthy summer visitors. Fortunately for today's visitors the best of the old was kept and restored.

A brief hiatus of activity surrounded the opening of an airfield at Crail for Royal Flying Corps training in July 1918, but this became superfluous with the Armistice and was ploughed under in 1919. In 1939 the Crail airfield was resurrected and became known as H.M.S. Jackdaw. This was a Fleet Air Arm training base and it is estimated the population of Crail doubled during its period of operation from 1940-47. The former airbase was used to train teenage naval recruits as H.M.S. Bruce from 1947-49, and as a transit camp for Black Watch soldiers being sent overseas from 1952-55. Finally, Crail aerodrome was used as a school for teaching Russian to the services during the dark days of the Cold War. This closed in 1960.

Crail's modest fishing fleet has halved in size during the last 70 years. There were 5 motor and 14 sail boats under 30' keel in 1928; there are now 10 small motor boats. The last herring were landed at Crail in 1943 and the remaining boats fish entirely for lobsters and partan crabs.

The nature of tourism in Scotland has changed radically in the last 30 years, with the inexorable decline of traditional seaside resorts. Today's tourists are heritage conscious, and Crail is the "jewel in the crown" of the East Neuk towns and villages. New housing has mushroomed on the margins of the town with a rise in population from 1,323 in 1971 to an estimated 1,653 in 1998. Further expansion is not desired by locals, and I'm inclined to agree. However, recent growth has guaranteed the sustainability of local services and amenities, and the future for Crail looks comfortable and assured.

The burgh arms of Crail on a postcards from the 1900s. The seven figures in the boat represent the seven incorporated trades of Crail, viz smiths, wrights, weavers, tailors, shoemakers, coopers and bakers. In 1938 Crail adopted the motto "At thy word I will let down the net" in Latin, which is taken from the Gospel of Luke.

A 1905 postcard view of the classic angle of Crail harbour. Probably the most photographed in Scotland, it has appeared on calendars, shortbread tins, souvenir ashtrays and fridge magnets, to name but a few. The hook shaped east pier on the right is the oldest, described as "new foundit" in 1610, and "old and ruinous, a great part of it beat down by a storm last winter" in 1707. It is said Dutch masons advised in its construction. The west pier was added by Robert Stevenson in 1821, and the pierheads of both were improved in 1871.

The Harbour, Crail

Crail had been a great station for the herring fishery in the early 18th century, but by 1791 it was reported the fishing had been in great decline for the past 50 years. Only 12 boats went from Crail to the herring in 1844, although its status as a curing station was briefly revived around 1855 when it supported 5 coopers, 119 packers and gutters, 10 net makers and 7 curers. In 1881 it had 34 boats and 50 fishermen, but this was the peak of its importance as an industry for the town. In 1928, 998 cwts of herring were landed at Crail, but no more after 1943. This view of the west pier is dated 1930. The house closest to the right of the picture, number 1 Temple Crescent, was destroyed by a bomb in 1941.

The size of the late 17th century customs house in the centre of this 1905 view recalls the faded mercantile importance of this once flourishing trading burgh. On the left lobsters or crabs are being loaded onto a cart, probably bound for the railway station and the London market. In 1791, it was reported some 20-25,000 lobsters were sent annually to the London market at £12.10 shillings per 1,000, but that a decade earlier the quantity had been almost twice as great.

In 1845 it was remarked that little shipping passed through Crail harbour excepting imports of coal for local use and exports of agricultural produce. Chief among these were potatoes, around 3,000 tons per annum being sent mainly to Newcastle and London. *Opposite*: Crail harbour 1911, white drift nets dry on the wall, indicating that it was taken during the winter herring season. The small yawl on the right of the big 'tattie' boat is the Janette, KY145.

Excavations at the Caiplie caves in the 19th century revealed a number of burials which were probably pre-Christian in date, and the remains of animal bones which suggested human habitation in the Bronze Age or earlier. The name is thought to derive from the Latin *capella*, meaning a church, and numerous incised crosses are to be found in the largest of the caves. These have been linked to St. Adrian and his followers who are said to have preached here in the 9th century. St. Adrian was allegedly the victim of a massacre of the monastic community on the Isle of May in 875 but it is more likely this is a later embellishment of the legend of the 7th century St. Ethernan, from whom Kilrenny derives its name. At the turn of the 20th century one of the caves was the home of an Irishman named Jimmy Gilligan, styled the Caiplie Hermit. In the paranoia which accompanied the outbreak of war in 1914, local yobs whipped themselves into a frenzy that Gilligan was an enemy spy and he was taunted, his home vandalised and one of his cats killed. Only the intervention of the local minister prevented a more serious incident, and the harmless recluse was left at peace.

A summer visitor strikes a pose in very new looking "holiday cla'es" in this 1930s snapshot showing the old Harbour Office and Shoregate. The house on the left of the harbour office has been fairly heavy handedly modernised in the 1960s. In the early 18th century Crail was such a busy fishing station that a figure of authority, usually an Edinburgh lawyer, was appointed by the Lord High Admiral to preside over the fishing, try offences and settle disputes among the fishermen. He had his own boat, and fired a gun to indicate the start and finish of the day's fishing, especially concerning observance of the Sabbath. Each boat had to pay a sum known as Admiral's Dues. All this was mere memory by 1790, but as late as the 1950s the Harbour Master had the right to exact 2*d* in share dues from all visiting vessels.

A morning gossip in this sunlit 1930s view of a virtually unchanged Shoregate. The houses on the left date from the 17th century. Note the projecting stones to protect the outside steps from damage by passing carts, known as pal or spur stanes.

Looking down Shoregate from the corner of St. Clair's Wynd in 1905. The old houses in the centre of the view were known as the Rockgate and were probably of 17th century date. They were unsentimentally swept away and replaced by Castle Terrace in 1907.

Apart from the uncluttered horizon this 1912 view of the east pier from Castle Walk remains virtually unchanged. The walkway was created in 1890 and still offers spectacular views across the firth as far as St. Abbs head. The sundial on the Castle Walk was removed from the harbour and re-erected here and has as its shaft part of a fossilised tree trunk.

The High Street looking idyllically peaceful and scarcely changed in a hundred years. The block of houses third from the right was built circa 1900 on the site of Tom Keay's brewery and are called the Maltings. The Keay family had been brewers in Crail since the 17th century.

Crail Post Office is on the left of this 1905 view, published by the postmaster John Scott, who produced around 40 different postcards of Crail in this series. The large tenement next door was extensively modernised and altered in 1907. Crail had a post office some time before 1755. In 1815 mail was brought from Leven in a horse drawn gig, while a running postman was the only link from Crail to St. Andrews. In 1845 the local minister lamented the discontinuation of this runner in 1829, complaining that letters to and from St. Andrews now didn't arrive until the next day, instead of within two hours as formerly!

A small sign on the left indicates John Scott's post office now boasts a public telephone in this 1909 view. Scott died in 1932 aged 86. He was local postmaster for 40 years and became a town council member in 1882. He served as a baillie for 20 years, and was provost of Crail from 1913 -21. Scott was succeeded as postmaster by George Nash upon his retirement in the 1920s.

W. Lindsay's grocery shop is in the right foreground of this unusual view of High Street, looking into West Green taken around 1910. These buildings date from the mid-19th century. In 1951 it was reported that Crail had 38 shops, all but three of which were located in the High Street and the town was largely self sufficient for all its shopping needs. Curiously no co-operative store ever established a branch here, although a van visited once a week from Anstruther.

The white house with its gable to the camera on the left of this 1905 view was demolished in the 1920s and replaced by the Commercial Bank of Scotland. The Golf Hotel on the right ran a horse drawn brake and wagonette which carried visitors to Balcomie for golf and bathing. In the 1920s these were superseded by two buses with canvas roofs run by the Crail Golfing Society. Another charabanc was operated by George Morris, and the rivalry between the two services led to some competitive and dangerous driving.

High Street looking west in 1909. The chemist's shop, beyond the hotel in the middle distance, is dated 1892. The Golf Hotel is thought to stand on the site of an inn dating back to the 14th century, although the present building dates from the early 18th. The former inn takes its name from being used as a meeting place by the members of the Crail Golfing Society which held its inaugural meeting here in 1786. The Golf was probably home to the first post office in Crail, although this cannot be confirmed. Its sharply corbelled corner suggests it was designed to allow the passage of a lot of traffic.

George Morris's Livery stables on the left of this 1905 view of St. Andrews Road have been replaced by new housing, but apart from the absence of traffic this scene is almost unchanged. In 1845 it was reported that a light van or wagon had daily carried goods and passengers from Crail to St. Andrews "for many years".

A Free Church congregation was established in Crail in 1843 and erected their first church in St. Andrews Road in 1845. In 1863 a United Presbyterian congregation added a third church to the town at the west end. In 1900 the United Free and United Presbyterian churches unified, and the St. Andrews Road church became known as the North U.F. church and its counterpart, the West U.F.. The North U.F. Church was demolished, and replaced by St. David's church in 1910. This view of the old church was taken a few years before its demolition in 1908.

The newly completed St. David's church was designed by J.D. Cairns and is shown on the left of this contemporary view. The congregation was merged with St. Mary's in 1954 and St. David's has since become a most impressive church hall. The cottages on the right were removed in 1913 when the site became part of Victoria Park. A gift from a former resident, Mr. George A. Gay of Hartford, Connecticut, the park was officially opened in July 1914. The ancient Sauchope Stone, an early Christian symbol stone which may date from the 8th century, was removed here in 1929 from its original location on the Crail to Balcomie road.

A pair of photographs from 1909 showing the Beech Walk and the continuation of the path into Bow Butts. The name Bow Butts is a relic from the 16th century when the area was used for archery practice by the local militia. The Beech Walk park was gifted to the town council of Crail by its three co-owners, George A. Gay of Connecticut, John W. Duncan of Coldrey and George D. White of Crail, in 1928 and formally opened as a public recreation ground the following year.

A bowling green for Crail was first proposed in 1891, and was opened for play in 1892. The members evidently took their game seriously, for in 1894 the committee decided the greenskeeper should be paid the not inconsiderable sum of one shilling and sixpence per night for catching worms! The green and pavilion in this 1909 view were replaced in 1925, and the old green was laid out as a children's play area after World War Two. The 1892 pavilion was converted to a public lavatory in 1936.

The tennis courts with St. David's church in the background, photographed in the late 1920s. It was proposed that a new bowling green and tennis courts be laid out in 1912, although the former was not created for another decade. In 1913 it was agreed the tennis courts should be extended to 42 yards in length so they could be flooded and used as artificial curling rinks in winter and Mr. Gordon Dow drew up plans for the tennis pavilion on the left of the picture. The tennis courts were opened in the summer of 1914.

In 1922 Crail Bowling Club bought the ground for a new bowling green and began fundraising for the cost of laying it out and the erection of a new pavilion. The new green was formally opened on 8 July 1925 by Provost Horsley. The station master's house can be seen in the background of this view which dates from the early 1950s.

Despite its popularity with summer visitors Crail was one of the last towns in Fife to receive a rail link. The Leven Railway was opened from Thornton to Leven in 1854, and extended to Kilconquhar as the East of Fife Railway three years later. In 1863 the line was further extended to Anstruther, but it was to take a further 20 years before the first train steamed into Crail. The L. & E.F.R. was absorbed into the North British Railway Company in 1877. By 1951 it was reported that although Sunday excursion trains brought numerous visitors to Crail, buses were cheaper, more frequent and better patronised. In 1964 the St. Andrews to Crail line was closed to freight, and on 6 September 1965 the whole line from St. Andrews to Leven was closed completely. Although the track and bridge have long gone, the buildings in this 1905 view are now part of a popular garden centre.

The horizontal view of the town hall and tollbooth dates from 1893, the vertical (*opposite*) from around 1910. The lower storeys of the tollbooth date from 1598 and it cost around 1,000 merks to erect the building, which had the primary function of being a prison with upper and lower cells. In 1702 the clock and bell were brought from the kirk steeple and installed in a wooden structure atop the prison. By 1776 this was much decayed and this part was reconstructed in stone as it is today. The bell was cast in Rotterdam and is dated 1520; it was tolled for curfew at 10 p.m. until quite recently. The adjoining town hall was rebuilt in 1814-15.

A 1904 postcard of Robert Kirkcaldy who was postman, church officer and town crier of Crail. He died in 1912 at the age of 84 and had lived in Crail for 50 years. He was described in his obituary as a man of remarkable memory who could quote extensive passages of poetry and prose, yet had an often childlike simplicity, and would devote himself to the humblest duty with gusto. His biographer wrote "Nothing perhaps awakened Robert's true sense of greatness than when he was out with the drum. Here he was seen at his best and it is bare justice to say that as a town crier he never had and is never likely to have an equal. Every word was declaimed with such an energy that one could hear him all over town". As postman, one of Robbie's duties was to collect a shilling from each family to provide a Christmas dinner for the poor. As a trick, he would remove his glass eye from its socket for the entertainment of local children. He was succeeded as bellman and town officer by Thomas Black, who retired in 1938 after 34 years service and was the last holder of the office.

Only the shaft of the Market Cross is original and dates from the 17th century; the steps and unicorn finial were additions made when the cross was restored and re-sited to mark Queen Victoria's Golden Jubilee in 1887. The house on the left next to the town hall in this 1905 view has been home since 1979 to Crail Museum. It has a marriage lintel of 1703, was rebuilt in 1876 and restored in 1946. The museum is run by the Crail Preservation Society, founded in 1959, and is entirely the product of voluntary endeavour. Its lively and informative displays rival those of many museums with professional staff and government funding.

Forelands Hotel, Marketgate pictured in the early 1930s. The name Forelands is derived from the broad market place where booths were formerly set up for the busy markets of Crail. The house was built in 1759 for Thomas Kingo and Barbara Ness, but is much altered with Victorian and Edwardian extensions. One of the most important occasions to be celebrated here was the 150th anniversary dinner of the Crail Golfing Society in 1936.

Kirkmay House in Marketgate was built in 1817 for James Inglis who owned the Kirkmay estate. In 1845 it was reported he had formerly operated a coal work on his estate with an engine to keep the workings pumped free of water, but had given up the enterprise. Fire and common clay were still dug in abundance on the estate and fire clay bricks and chimney cans were manufactured on the Kirkmay estate and shipped to Dundee, Arbroath and other towns to a considerable extent.

The parish church of Crail was gifted to the Culdees in the 11th century, but came under the control of the priors of St. Andrews in the 12th, although its revenues were the property of the convent of Haddington. The tower and nave are believed to date at least in part from around 1200. It was dedicated by David de Bernham in 1243 to St. Maelrutha of Applecross. The stone spire was added in the early 16th century, possibly contemporary with the Dutch bell of 1520 which was later transferred to the tollbooth. The body of the kirk was extensively remodelled in 1815 to plans by Robert Balfour. This view dates from 1904; the war memorial gates were added in 1921.

The interior of St. Mary's parish church has changed considerably since this photograph was taken in 1907. Knox preached here in 1559 and at his exhortations the congregation attacked the statuary, stained glass and many altars of the church as he spoke. From 1648 to 1661 James Sharp was minister here, and it was during his first year the parish registers were begun to be kept. The pulpit was resited in 1936 when the arch behind was filled by a huge pipe organ, acquired second hand from a large house in Kirkcaldy. The pulpit and some of the box pews were removed during a major refurbishment in 1963 as they had become infested with woodworm. Notwithstanding this, many of the pews still bear the names of the local well-to-do families from the 18th Century.

The Nursing Home was built in the 1900s as a boarding house by the name of Miramar. In the 1930s it became a convalescent and retirement home which was well respected by the 1950s. Note the summer houses which could rotate on rails to catch the sun at all times of the day and evening.

Rumford remains virtually identical from this view of 1910. The pair of houses beyond the projecting gable on the left were built in the 17th century as the burgh's poor house. They were restored in 1961 by the National Trust and were the first houses in their revolving restoration scheme, whereby properties were restored and resold into private hands to finance future restoration projects.

The building with gothic arched windows at the apex of this 1909 view of the Nethergate was built in 1824 as the burgh school and the building was removed to this site from the entrance to St. Mary's church when the new school opened in St. Andrews Road in 1889. The architect is believed to have been Robert Balfour. The former school became the public library and latterly shared its home with the Royal British Legion, which took over the whole premises when the library transferred to the town hall in the 1990s.

Jackson's Marine Hotel in Nethergate photographed from the rear shortly after opening in 1903. Only the Golf Hotel remains of the Crail's four big hotels extant in 1951; the others, including the Marine have been converted to private houses or flats.

A deserted view of Nethergate looking east in 1900. Beyond Downie Terrace on the right of the street are fragments of old walls which are believed to be part of a 16th century nunnery. Human remains were found here when the site was being levelled in the 1870s. The heavily harled barrel shaped doocot by the footpath to Roome Bay is the last vestige of this religious house. The nearby grassy area is called the Briery Braes, thought to be a corruption of Priory Braes recalling the site of the now lost St. Rufus priory which stood on the foreshore. The last traces of this, a gable wall with lancet window, were washed away around 1801. The Nethergate Port stood east of where Downie Terrace was built, recalling the ancient gates of the burgh.

Downie Terrace looking towards Roome Bay in 1905. The construction of these houses was a speculative venture by Mr. Downie in 1878 to provide seaside residences for summer visitors, for which he received the freedom of the burgh. The Priory, a baronial inspired villa was added in 1915. The houses in Roome Bay Crescent on the horizon are roughly contemporary with this view and have been joined by many bungalows.

The first bungalows in Roome Bay Avenue were completed by the Murrayfield Estate Company of Edinburgh in 1925, along what had been known as the Double Dykes Road. The same developer built further bungalows in Balcomie Road in 1932.

The Sauchope links caravan park, pictured in 1959. Sauchope was the original course of the Crail Golfing Society, founded in 1786. They played over 8 holes, with competitions played over two or three rounds. After a period of suspension through lack of interest in the 1850s the club was resurrected in 1859 with an 8 hole course at Balcomie. Sauchope links was improved in 1890 and increased to 9 holes; the Balcomie course to 18 holes in 1899. Both courses were requisitioned for military use during the last war, and the links at Sauchope were never restored to golfing use. The caravan site was created around 1950.

Ploughing at Balcomie Castle, postmarked 1910. James Learmonth of Clatto was granted the lands of Balcomie in 1526 but the earliest surviving parts of the castle date from the second half of the 16th century. The surviving portion is the south west corner of a U-plan block with a four storey main block flanked by wings on either side.

The white houses on the right of this mid 1930s view of Fife Ness were the Kilmining Cottages, which are now abandoned and ruinous. The wall a short distance to the left contains blocked up windows and doors indicating older abandoned houses. Kilmining, it has been suggested, may be the site of an early Christian settlement, the Kil or cell of Monan, linked also with St. Monans. Over 30 stone lined graves were uncovered near here in the 19th century. There was once a substantial community of crofter fishermen at Fife Ness, it even had a horse fair as late as 1710, a privilege of the Learmonths of Balcomie.

Teeing off at Balcomie in 1948. A nine hole course was opened at Balcomie in 1895, with a wooden pavilion obtained second hand from the tennis club, which can be seen on the left of the picture. Four years later the course was extended to 18 holes with advice on layout from Tom Morris of St. Andrews. The popularity of the game waned during WWI and the town council acquired the lease of Balcomie to ensure the course would survive. Sunday golf was banned in 1918 and remained a recurring issue at council meetings, eventually leading to a plebiscite of rate payers in 1935, when 243 voted in favour of golf on Sundays to 31 against. The clubhouse in the photograph was erected in 1904 and extended in 1935 and 1970. The Crail Golfing Society bought the course from the town council in 1973. Major extensions to the clubhouse in 2002 have all but hidden the old building.

A rare postcard view of lifeboat drill at Fife Ness circa 1905. The lifeboat *George Paterson* arrived at Crail station on 6 November 1884 when a crowd of 2,000 assembled to witness the event. This lifeboat remained in service until 1910 when it was replaced by the *Elizabeth Kay*, which was finally withdrawn from service in 1923. The old lifeboat house at Balcomie is now used as a store by the Golfing Society.

The coastguard visited Fife Ness with a view to establishing a station in 1903 and this was operational two years later. This 1907 card was sent by H.W., one of the coastguard stationed here, to a colleague at Rosehearty near Fraserburgh. He says "This is a photo of our station, the best of it is on the card. The mast is obscured but it is lowermast and topmast 65 feet."

A youthful troop of auxiliary coastguard photographed at Fife Ness in April 1915. The young volunteers provided extra eyes to scan the firth for enemy activity and ensure the welfare of our own shipping. When not engaged in work of such national gravity, these lads seem to have invented skiffle music in their spare time!